SPOTLIGHT ON CIVIC ACTION

THE IMPORTANCE OF JURY SERVICE

KAISA WALKER

NEW YORK

Published in 2018 by The Rosen Publishing Group, Inc.
29 East 21st Street, New York, NY 10010

Editor: Elizabeth Krajnik
Book Design: Michael Flynn
Interior Layout: Rachel Rising

Photo Credits: Cover, sturti/E+/Getty Images; p. 5 David Young-Wolff/The Image Bank/Getty Images; pp. 7, 11, 25 Courtesy of the Library of Congress; p. 9 Hulton Archive/Hulton Archive/Getty Images; p. 13 (main) Tracey Helmboldt/Shutterstock.com; p. 13 (inset) Michelle Milano/Shutterstock.com; pp. 14, 15 PNC/Photodisc/Getty Images; p. 16 Rawpixel.com/Shutterstock.com; p. 17 Africa Studio/Shutterstock.com; p. 19 Cathy Murphy/Hulton Archive/Getty Images; p. 21 sirtravelalot/Shutterstock.com; p. 22 holbox/Shutterstock.com; p. 23 Courtesy of United States Courts; pp. 26, 27 Portland Press Herald/Portland Press Herald/Getty Images; p. 29 moodboard/Brand X Pictures/Getty Images.

Cataloging-in-Publication Data

Names: Walker, Kaisa.
Title: The importance of jury service / Kaisa Walker.
Description: New York : PowerKids Press, 2018. | Series: Spotlight on civic action | Includes index.
Identifiers: ISBN 9781538327951 (pbk.) | ISBN 9781508164036 (library bound) | ISBN 9781538328071 (6 pack)
Subjects: LCSH: Jury--United States--Juvenile literature.
Classification: LCC KF8972.W35 2018 | DDC 347.73'52--dc23

Manufactured in China

CPSIA Compliance Information: Batch #BW18PK For further information contact Rosen Publishing, New York, New York at 1-800-237-9932.

CONTENTS

WHAT'S A JURY? 4

GRAND JURIES 6

A HISTORY OF JURIES 8

JURIES IN THE UNITED STATES 10

SELECTION PROCESS 12

BECOMING A JUROR 16

A CONSTITUTIONAL RIGHT 18

CHECKS AND BALANCES 20

THE U.S. COURT SYSTEM 22

CITIZEN EMPOWERMENT 24

RESOLVING DISPUTES PEACEFULLY 26

GET EDUCATED! 30

GLOSSARY 31

INDEX 32

PRIMARY SOURCE LIST 32

WEBSITES 32

CHAPTER ONE

WHAT'S A JURY?

A jury is a group of citizens chosen to hear the facts and decide the **verdict** of a case in a court of law. These people are called jurors. In the United States, there are two different kinds of juries—trial juries, or petit juries, and grand juries.

Trial juries are made up of 6 to 12 people. In civil cases, the jury listens to the evidence the lawyers present to decide whether the defendant, or person being sued, is liable, or responsible. If so, the jury may also decide what the penalty will be.

Criminal trial juries are made up of 12 people. They listen to evidence presented against the defendant to help them decide whether the defendant is guilty. If the defendant is found guilty, the judge usually decides what the defendant's punishment will be.

Civil and criminal cases are different. Civil cases are legal disputes between two or more parties. Criminal cases occur when the government charges someone with a crime.

CHAPTER TWO

GRAND JURIES

Grand juries can have between 16 and 23 people. In the United States, grand juries don't determine if a person is guilty of committing a crime. The jury listens to the evidence against the defendant and determines whether there is probable cause, or enough evidence, to indicate that this person may be guilty. If the jury says there's probable cause, then the person will be put on trial.

A grand jury's purpose is to determine whether a trial is needed. This means that the grand jury process itself is not a trial. There's no judge present and no verdict. Grand jury proceedings, unlike trial jury proceedings, aren't open to the public. The defendant and their lawyers aren't allowed to appear before the jury. Some states have civil grand juries, which often look into the operations of local governments.

In 1913, the Arcadia Hotel fire in Boston, Massachusetts, resulted in 28 deaths. A grand jury later visited the site, which is shown here. The grand jury's job was to determine whether the fire was accidental or set on purpose.

CHAPTER THREE

A HISTORY OF JURIES

Scholars often disagree about the origin of juries. Some say that juries started in England. Others say the idea was brought to England by Norman invaders in 1066. Juries at that time were made up of neighborhood people who had witnessed crimes or injustices. These people were the ones who decided if a person was guilty because they had seen the actual events. As towns grew larger, the role of juries changed. Juries were presented with evidence and had to decide the facts under the common law.

As the British Empire spread across the world, British **customs** were adopted in new colonies. In a similar way, Napoleon Bonaparte, the emperor of France (1804–1815), spread the jury's popular use throughout mainland Europe. Today, however, juries aren't used or are rarely used in many countries throughout the world.

Although many countries no longer use juries, the United States has the most jury trials in the world.

CHAPTER FOUR

JURIES IN THE UNITED STATES

In the United States, citizens have the right to a trial by jury. Some countries, such as England, consider trial by jury a **privilege**. Because the United States is composed of former British colonies, much of its legal system is based off England's. However, in the years since the United States became an independent country, its judicial system has changed.

American juries have a greater impact than juries in countries such as England and Canada. Juries in some states have the ability to decide whether a person should receive the death penalty. They may also decide how long a person's sentence will be if they committed a serious crime.

American colonists built their own judicial system to fit their needs. Over time, juries have become an identifying institution of the United States.

The 1735 **libel** trial of John Peter Zenger, a New York newspaper printer, helped give rise to a one-of-a-kind American judicial system. This trial set the stage for a larger role for juries in the future United States.

CHAPTER FIVE

SELECTION PROCESS

The selection process for jurors in America became very important after the American Revolution. People realized that the means by which jurors were selected affected people's individual freedoms. Before the war, English leaders made sure people who were supportive of England were chosen as jurors to prevent colonist uprisings. To keep this issue from happening, the newly independent country focused greatly on how its jurors would be selected.

Today, juries are a cross section of society. This means that they are made up of people of different backgrounds. There are two steps in jury selection. The first step is random selection. In random selection, the state or federal district pulls the names of potential jurors off lists of citizens, such as people who are registered voters, hold a driver's license, or receive unemployment benefits.

JURORS REPORT HERE

YOU REPORT FOR JURY DUTY

DETACH AT PERFORATION FOR JUROR BADGE

JUROR

UNITED STATES DISTRICT COURT

US Dist

LOCATION:

DATE: Mo

TIME

JUROR

PH(

DETACH

People called for jury duty receive a notice in the mail. This notice includes the date they must be present in court. Unless a person has a good reason to miss jury duty, it is very important to go.

When someone reports to the courthouse for jury duty, they must go through a process known as voir dire, which is French for "to speak the truth." Voir dire is when the judge and lawyers associated with the case interview potential jurors. They ask the jurors questions about their backgrounds and beliefs and if they have any biases that might affect their decision.

Jurors who make it through voir dire will be sworn in for the trial. Everyone else is excused. The jurors then take an oath by repeating words stated by the judge or the clerk.

Lawyers can object to jurors in two ways. A challenge for cause is when a lawyer objects to a juror because something about their background or interview indicated that they could be biased in the case. A **peremptory** challenge allows a lawyer to object to a juror without giving a cause for doing so. However, lawyers can't object to a juror because of their race or because they're male or female.

CHAPTER SIX

BECOMING A JUROR

To become a juror, an individual must be a U.S. citizen. They must be at least 18 years old and have lived in their judicial district for at least one year. Individuals must also be able to read and write English well enough to fill out the juror qualification form.

Certain individuals aren't required to serve as jurors. These people include members of the armed forces on active duty, professional firefighters and police officers, and people who hold public offices in government, such as senators and representatives in Congress.

An individual can't serve as a juror if they have certain mental or physical conditions. If a person has been charged with a **felony** that could result in going to prison for more than a year or if they have been found guilty of a felony, they can't serve as a juror. However, in some states, people whose voting rights have been restored after they've served their time for a crime can become jurors.

CHAPTER SEVEN

A CONSTITUTIONAL RIGHT

If accused of a crime, each American citizen has the right to be tried by a jury of their peers. This right is outlined in the Sixth and Seventh Amendments to the U.S. Constitution. The jury selection process aims to find jurors that represent people from different backgrounds. This keeps juries from introducing bias in their decision about the case.

Sometimes juries aren't truly composed of a defendant's peers. In 1950, Pete Hernández was accused and found guilty of murdering a man in Jackson County, Texas. His lawyer, Gustavo García, appealed, arguing that the people who chose the jurors **discriminated** against potential Mexican American jurors. The case of *Hernández v. State of Texas* went to the U.S. Supreme Court, where the justices required Hernández to be retried by a new jury selected without discrimination against Mexican Americans.

UNITED FARM WORKERS' 1,000 MILE MARCH
CALIFORNIA, 1975
MEXICAN AMERICAN CIVIL RIGHTS MOVEMENT

The Supreme Court ruled that Hernández had "the right to be **indicted** and tried by juries from which all members of his class are not **systematically** excluded." This was a huge victory for the Mexican American civil rights movement of the 1940s through the 1970s.

CHAPTER EIGHT

CHECKS AND BALANCES

There are three branches of the U.S. government: the executive branch (the president, vice president, cabinet, and others), the legislative branch (the Senate and the House of Representatives), and the judicial branch (the Supreme Court and other federal courts). When the Founding Fathers outlined how the government would operate, they included special rules that allow each branch to check the others to make sure no one branch could become too powerful. This is known as a separation of powers.

Juries are part of the larger reach of the judicial branch. Even though the Supreme Court doesn't have jurors, juries at the lower state and federal levels are essential to a strong judicial branch, which is needed for the system of checks and balances to be successful. A well-chosen jury that represents all corners of American society is needed for a trial to be fair.

Trials by jury prevent the government from **oppressing** its people. Jury trials give absolute power to the citizens of the jury to make their decision. When the people hold the power, it is less likely that the government will get too powerful.

CHAPTER NINE

THE U.S. COURT SYSTEM

In the federal court system, juries are only present in district courts. The United States has 94 district, or trial, courts. Each state—as well as Washington, D.C., Puerto Rico, the Northern Mariana Islands, Guam, and the U.S. Virgin Islands—has at least one district court. In each district court, there's a district judge, whose job it is to try the case, and a jury, whose job it is to decide the case.

SUPREME COURT BUILDING
WASHINGTON, D.C.

Each of the 12 regional circuits has one appellate court. There's also the United States Court of Appeals for the Federal Circuit. This court has nationwide control, but only hears certain cases.

These 94 district courts are organized into 12 regional circuits. There are also 13 federal **appellate** courts. Appellate courts are higher than district courts. They make sure the law was properly applied in the district courts. Each U.S. federal court of appeals has three judges and doesn't use a jury.

The Supreme Court is the highest court in the U.S. court system. Supreme Court cases must have originated in federal court or deal with federal law.

CHAPTER TEN

CITIZEN EMPOWERMENT

Imagine you're sitting in a courtroom after a criminal trial has taken place. The jury has made its decision and they've found the defendant guilty of a serious crime. You don't agree with the jury's decision. However, there's nothing you can do. Now imagine you were a member of that same jury. You had the power to voice your opinion about the evidence that the defense and prosecution presented to you.

Your job as a juror was to decide what was factual and to apply the law as the judge had advised. Sometimes the evidence in a case conflicts and it becomes the job of the jury to decide what really happened. Your role as a juror was empowering because you got to have a voice in the judicial branch of the government.

The people pictured here are members of the jury that found Albert B. Fall—secretary of the interior under President Warren G. Harding—guilty of bribery on October 25, 1929.

CHAPTER ELEVEN

RESOLVING DISPUTES PEACEFULLY

Trials by jury are just one way to resolve disputes peacefully. Many people have seen movies and TV shows in which there are trials, but these are usually much more dramatic than most real-life trials.

Matthew Nichols, pictured here, delivers his opening statement in the trial of Gregory Nisbet. Nisbet is the landlord of an apartment building where six people died in a fire in 2014.

NISBET TRIAL,
CUMBERLAND COUNTY COURTHOUSE,
PORTLAND, OREGON

Trials happen in stages. The first stage is the pretrial motions. In this stage, lawyers for each party often argue that certain pieces of information should be taken out of the trial or not be mentioned to the jury or that certain witnesses should not be allowed to speak.

Next, the jury members are selected. (See Chapter 5.) After the jury has been selected and sworn in, lawyers from each side make opening statements, which outline the evidence that will be presented in the trial. Opening statements are not meant to be arguments about the facts of the case.

After each party's lawyer has delivered their opening statement, the lawyers will present the evidence. First, the prosecution presents the evidence against the defendant. This is when witnesses are called to **testify**. Then, the defendant's lawyer will present their evidence.

In civil cases, the jury is sent out of the room at this point. The judge and both parties' lawyers will discuss what law should be applied to the case to help the jury make its decision. The jury comes back into the courtroom and the lawyers deliver their closing arguments to the jury.

Before the jury leaves for deliberation, the judge instructs them on what legal standards they should consider, as discussed previously by the judge and lawyers. This is called the jury charge. In criminal trials, closing arguments are made before the jury charge.

After the jury has deliberated—which can take minutes, hours, and even days—the jury returns to the courtroom to deliver the verdict. In criminal cases, the jury will either find the defendant guilty or not guilty. In civil cases, the jury will determine if the defendant is liable. The defendant has the right to appeal the verdict in a higher court.

CHAPTER TWELVE

GET EDUCATED!

Understanding why juries are so important requires a lot of background information. Sometimes, trials result in a hung jury, which means that the jury is unable to reach a verdict because the members can't agree. If the jury is hung, the judge will declare a mistrial. A mistrial means that there will need to be a new trial with a new jury.

A trial by jury is an American constitutional right. Showing up for jury duty helps make sure all Americans can exercise their rights. You have a duty to your country to help your fellow citizens in this manner. People should appreciate that the United States is a country in which trials by jury exist. Juries allow the people to act as part of the judicial branch.

GLOSSARY

appellate (uh-PEH-luht) Of or relating to appeals, or the legal action by which a court case is brought to a higher court for review, or the power to hear appeals.

custom (KUH-stuhm) An action or way of behaving that is traditional among the people in a certain group or place.

discriminate (dis-KRIH-muh-nayt) To treat people unequally based on class, race, or religion.

felony (FEH-luh-nee) A very serious crime.

indict (in-DYT) To formally decide someone should go on trial for a crime.

libel (LY-buhl) The publication of a false statement that hurts a person's reputation.

oppress (uh-PRES) To control or rule in a harsh or cruel way.

peremptory (puh-REMP-tuh-ree) Having to do with a command, ruling, or decision that does not allow for questioning or debate.

privilege (PRIV-lij) A right or liberty granted as a favor or benefit to some and not others.

systematically (si-stuh-MAA-tih-kuh-lee) In a careful, planned-out way.

testify (TES-tuh-fy) To speak or answer questions in a court of law.

verdict (VER-dikt) The decision reached by a jury.

INDEX

A
American Revolution, 12
appellate courts, 23

B
Bonaparte, Napoleon, 8
British Empire, 8

C
Canada, 10
challenge for cause, 15
Constitution, U.S., 18
Court of Appeals for the Federal
    Circuit, U.S, 23

D
district courts, 22, 23

E
England, 8, 9, 10, 12
executive branch, 20

F
France, 8

G
García, Gustavo, 18

H
Hernández, Pete, 18, 19
Hernández v. State of Texas, 18
House of Representatives, 20
hung jury, 30

J
judicial branch, 20, 24, 30
jury charge, 28

L
legislative branch, 20

M
mistrial, 30

O
opening statements, 26, 27, 28

P
peremptory challenge, 15
pretrial motions, 27
probable cause, 6

R
regional circuits, 23

S
Senate, 20
Seventh Amendment, 18
Sixth Amendment, 18
Supreme Court, U.S., 18, 19, 20, 22,
    23

U
United States, 4, 6, 9, 10, 11, 22, 23,
    30

V
voir dire, 14

Z
Zenger, John Peter, 11

PRIMARY SOURCE LIST

Page 7
Grand jury at Arcadia hotel fire. Photograph. ca. 1913. Now kept at the Library of Congress Prints and Photographs Division Washington, D.C.

Page 11
Andrew Hamilton defending John Peter Zenger in court, 1734–35. Wood engraving. ca. 1877 and 1896. Now kept at the Library of Congress Prints and Photographs Division Washington, D.C.

Page 25
Jury that found Albert B. Fall guilty of bribery. Photograph. Created September 25, 1929, by Harris & Ewing. Now kept at the Library of Congress Prints and Photographs Division Washington, D.C.

WEBSITES

Due to the changing nature of Internet links, PowerKids Press has developed an online list of websites related to the subject of this book. This site is updated regularly. Please use this link to access the list: www.powerkidslinks.com/sociv/jury